Praise for *Realia*

Ping-ponging back and forth ⬚⬚⬚⬚⬚⬚⬚⬚⬚⬚⬚
a poetic voice that is helpful, i⬚⬚⬚⬚⬚⬚⬚⬚⬚⬚
Trussler takes in the rubble of ⬚⬚⬚⬚⬚⬚⬚⬚⬚⬚
manifesto for the anti-sublime ⬚⬚⬚⬚⬚⬚⬚⬚⬚
hallucinations). Every thing is not a thing but "vibrant matter"
and not particularly kind but more or less loyal to "juddering"
humans, or so we like to think. The frightening are everywhere.
And then the reader comes upon the extraordinary poetic essay
for Katherine Mansfield. *Realia* is fierce and tender.

Tim Lilburn
author of *Numinous Seditions: Interiority and Climate Change*

Michael Trussler's *Realia* is a hefty thing, offering a curious lyric
that approaches perception head-on, flickering between seeing
and comprehending. When and how does observation sink in?
At what point does the very act of witness alter what is being seen?

rob mclennan
author of *the book of smaller*

Michael Trussler's *Realia* lingers at the fringes of universality –
questioning lived and unlived realities. *Beyond the end of this sentence
I understand almost nothing*, Trussler confesses to his readers,
yet he has built a house made of language that levels us.
These poems and poetic essays hold a magnifying glass up to
what is urgent, what is divergent, what strips and renders us.
Trussler's gift is nonsensical storytelling; his confessional
grief and madness a promise to his readers that
the story will indeed fall off the bone.

Adrienne Gruber
author of *Monsters, Martyrs, and Marionettes*

realia

realia POETRY

michael trussler

radiant press

Editor: gillian harding-russell
Cover art: Jordan Baraniecki
Book and cover design: Tania Wolk, Third Wolf Studio
Printed and bound in Canada at Friesens, Altona, MB

The publisher gratefully acknowledges the support of
Creative Saskatchewan, the Canada Council for the Arts and SK Arts.

Library and Archives Canada Cataloguing in Publication

Title: Realia / Michael Trussler.
Names: Trussler, Michael, 1960- author.
Description: Includes bibliographical references.
Identifiers: Canadiana (print) 2024034443X | Canadiana (ebook) 20240344448
ISBN 9781998926039 (softcover)
ISBN 9781998926046 (EPUB)
Subjects: LCGFT: Poetry.
Classification: LCC PS8639.R89 R43 2024 | DDC C811/.6—dc23

radiant press
Box 33128 Cathedral PO
Regina, SK S4T 7X2
info@radiantpress.ca
www.radiantpress.ca

To Jakob

Realia, first used in the late 19th century, is still mostly used in the classroom by teachers, especially foreign language teachers. Also used in library cataloguing (in reference to such bizarre objects as an author's hair and teeth donated posthumously) the term occasionally finds its way into other contexts as well. You might, for example, hear of someone putting "realia"-objects that represent present-day life-in a time capsule. "Realia" is also sometimes used philosophically to distinguish real things from the theories about them-a meaning that dates to the early 19th century. "Realia" is one of those plural formations without a corresponding singular form. Like "memorabilia" ("memorable things" or "mementos"), "juvenilia" ("works produced in an artist's or author's youth"), and "marginalia" ("marginal notes or embellishments"), it incorporates the Latin plural ending "-ia."

—adapted from *Merriam-Webster*

How does someone stay attached to life while repudiating the world of bad objects?

Lauren Berlant, *On the Inconvenience of Other People*

"A third element in the shaping of poems, the completion of canvases, is the enactment of a floaty, drifting, non-compulsive, multi-channel mimesis in an effort to receive and replicate the real as it appears in the charged, affect-rich atmosphere of contemplative attention."

Tim Lilburn, *Numinous Seditions: Interiority and Climate Change*

CONTENTS

When Eyelids

The two images could hardly be more different: Caspar David Friedrich's *The Monk by the Sea,* and Kevin Carter's photograph of a starving child in Sudan, nearly collapsed on the ground and being observed by a nearby vulture. Friedrich's painting, once owned by Fredrick Wilhelm III, now waits in the Alte Nationalgalerie in Berlin; the photograph, originally published by the *New York Times* and *Johannesburg Mail & Guardian* on March 26, 1993, is easily accessed online.

Looking into the painting not long ago, I realized that, without the monk staring into the waves, the painting was merely a seascape. A powerful and very disturbing seascape certainly—its extraordinary fraying of colours summoning Rothko—but the monk's presence completely alters the painting's dynamics. Gazing along the beach, across the waves and then taking in the human figure who, facing away from us, is himself opened to the sea, I felt my mind stumble, the picture slowly and suddenly erasing my ego, leaving my mind nearly empty except for the subdued ferocity of the scene taking up its own rhythm inside, something nearly unknown inside responding to the blackening merger of waves and sky. The harsh flicker of white caps and gulls.

Carter's image has flashed by many times—I can hardly remember the occasions—but I didn't subscribe to any newspaper in 1993 and so have no memory of when the photograph originally became public.

When Kleist saw Friedrich's painting in a gallery, he wrote: *"There can be nothing sadder or more desolate in the world than this place."* I don't know what Kleist felt when he took this painting in...but

I wonder what it meant to have lived in a world in which it made sense to locate that particularly terrible desolation primarily within art and how such a thing can still make the mind move towards it and recoil.

Who can touch what Lear holds when he carries Cordelia?

Now, the viciously uncanny. The monk in the painting is a *Rückenfigur*, that is, a figure seen from the back, an optical technique that Kleist would have recognized as a means to allow the viewer to move inside the painting[1], but when one conceives of the vulture as a non-human being who faces the child and could take in an observer of the photograph, a creature that would definitely have seen Carter move in its direction, one becomes agitated to realise that the bird is itself a kind of *Rückenfigur*. How can we reconcile the postures of bird and monk? The similarity between the two images—one made in the early nineteenth century, the other taken by a member of the late twentieth-century Bang-Bang Club—incurs fascination and revulsion. The irreconcilable violence of the actual summons nausea as much as the recognition of repeated patterns elicits curiosity. When Griselda Pollock asks—"Did Carter know what his photographer's eye longed for while he waited, watching bird and child?"—she elicits the innate tug of form, the artist's eye alert to composition and exactitude. Its repetition through centuries and passage through individual, separately-joined minds. Friedrich's and

---

1 Though as many critics observe, one can't actually gain a footing in the painting. Clemens Brentano provides this early commentary: "It is magnificent to stand in infinite solitude on the seashore.... Part of this feeling is the fact that one has made one's way there and yet must go back...that one sees nothing to support life and yet senses the voice of life in the sigh of the waves, the murmur of the air, the passing clouds and the cry of the birds.... But this is impossible in front of the picture, and what I should have found in the picture itself, I found only between myself and the picture, namely a claim my heart made on the picture and the picture's rejection of me."

Carter's. Ours. Kleist continues: "The picture, with its two or three mysterious subjects (monk, dune, sea) lies there like an apocalypse, as if it were thinking Edward Young's "Night Thoughts" and since it has, in its uniformity and boundlessness, no foreground but the frame, it is as if one's eyelids had been cut off." Hyperbole certainly, taming the sublime by turning it into verbal excess, but accurate enough in certain ways. A further question starts deepening as one would like to know whether Kleist would find himself with eyelids clipped away if he'd instead been taking in the vulture and the child, not something we can determine with certainty,[2] but one can say that our civilization's addiction to images spits out the child, places the seascape on T-shirts for kids and grownups you can order online. And the carnage in Sudan continues thirty years later; the child's identity is unknown to those of us who type the words to do a Google search for the photograph.

The syntax of images twists, and there are disturbing, connecting threads everywhere.[3]

Both Carter and Kleist died by suicide and the poet's memorial is near the Wannsee villa where the Nazis formalized the Final Solution on January 20, 1942. Who knows what was in Kleist's mind when he forced himself away from the painting and left the gallery? But those selections at Auschwitz-Birkenau—when the transports arrived and the Nazis separated who would be gassed

---

2 Kleist's short story "The Earthquake in Chile" would suggest however that the natural sublime, an earthquake, can reveal the violence which people will inflict upon each other to reinforce their ideologies.

3 As I type these words, people in Turkey and Syria are mourning the loss of over 24,000 victims to last week's earthquake. From the safe distance of Saskatchewan, one can send donations, but it is entirely unclear to me how one should engage with such a disaster in a prose poem.

from those sentenced to slave labour—does anyone alive today even know how many took place?—those selections render Kleist's perception into something that threatens the mind. If we can't determine how Kleist would have responded to a famine created by people, we do know that Carter thought of his own daughter when he took the picture and he then helped the starving child to a relief station and that he was awarded the Pulitzer Prize for the image. He couldn't have known, though, who would have found him after asphyxiating himself in his pick-up truck by carbon monoxide poisoning in the suburbs of the city in which he was born.

The sheer affliction of the unknown, homeless child made visible through Carter's photography and then circulated through the media, the intrusion of the actual biological creature that was the vulture—this constellation of realities disrupts and then both trashes-and-reconfigures the Romantic sublime. The child didn't choose; the solitary Romantic does. I don't wish to exploit either the child or Carter, nor diminish the painting that Kleist saw. It's simply that it's difficult to see either image separately: they call out to us, now in the twenty-first century, and also perhaps, very slowly, to each other.

Shambolic Rehearsals

Reality isn't so much a model to be slavishly copied
as a vocabulary to be reshaped.

–Jed Perl, "Colors in Conversation"

Nobody Move

A miniature wooden dock shining in
the mist is my spirit's alma mater.

Something's gone. Beyond the end of
this sentence I understand almost nothing.

The rest has been tinkering. Or
torched. Share & shock alike. A

rehabilitated and endless rage
must be at play. On the precipice

of tears, conventional daylight is gooey
and very quickly and plainly becoming

the second most destroyed city on earth.
Standing in for centuries,
                              IV tubes are not people—

An Octogenarian Armchair First Set Out

to invent a new form of martial arts, to be a shaman of
sorts, to be a perpetual biomorphic with a taste for torches
and handmade guns. Gems too. Sapphires mostly. But gave

it up at forty. Chose instead stop motion restorative
ecology ping-ponging as memento mori but that hobby
required mitochondrial psychology and lessons in

The most accurate portrayal of contemporary reality is the graph.
Christophe Bonneuil and Jean-Baptiste Fressoz chart socio-economic
and earth system trends in *The Shock of the Anthropocene*: 24 graphs
displaying data from population growth to the rise in international
tourism to tropical forest loss. Each a hockey stick, spanning 1750 to
2010. Each graph the record, not of Hegel's ever-expanding World
Spirit, but of a collapsing totality that beggars the imagination. What
is it that allows our individual experience to be amplified *just so* over
the centuries to have moved us to where we are now, in a situation in
which the present is barely present in the present because the future
is rewriting and rewiring everything?

extinct Barbie Doll arrangement. How could that happen?
Sit down. Full disclosure. Much of this story's being told
by words that have passed their use-before-date. Digital

menagerie. Outlier. Rare metal mining. Prefrontal cortex
activity. A solid frenzied week of. The illicit microplastic
catacombs between us and them. Numbers learning to riot.

Your call.

What Is

the collective noun for folks living one
day away from what they most fear? In how

many languages can you convincingly
learn to laugh? Open your skin to wet
bulb heat waves performing *mise en scène?* Just in
today: even Arnold Schwarzenegger's a fan
of Seneca. Just
landed. Here at last. Wow, there
are these amazing connections reappearing
people once made. If I see

you later, baby-talk
something inscrutable to me:
                                  spool-y-spin
deliberate reincarnation, cute money-mingling, socially-
sequacious whale-and-squid-watching, the safe &
sophisticated bits. Beget order, beget
the self-evident. *Picus viridis.* The laughing
European woodpecker. Mischief. All of
the above,
                    aloft. The diagnosis. The fold-out
cot in a gymnasium. Everything else

gone. Aphasia. Listen. Genres
vivify

a need for which no alternative method exists.

Science Fiction

Observation:

It was a beautiful, sequestered hallway in May. Moreover, Franklin gulls emit different spheres of thought depending upon the season.

Hypothesis:

Authors must make choices, yet the primal scene isn't one of dividing curtains or diverging continents. At the root of everything is simply: I hate seeing you like this—

Prediction:

History = milkshake duck.

Experiment:

Abandoning my puny studies to stumble elsewhere, refusing my debt to the hard-wired acrobatics of the future ←

Confirmation:

What awaits?

For a week or more, I've been stymied by the invention of the electric toilet seat, its aura, and the Anna's hummingbirds kept alive by an ocean poet who heated sugar water each half hour during a sudden freeze and I can't grasp what it means to draw from life or what I've heard about St. Francis granting a bat the gift of eyesight to enable it to (better) go hunting—

A Grammar of Spontaneity

1.
Make yourself at home.

2.
Anatomically opulent and gritty as amateur
P=O=R=N=A=M=E=N=T=A=R=Y but
                                        incapable of
literal copy, the human amygdala is fond
of being the final apparition
in Proust's aquarium to

3.
steadily disappear—

4.
Struggling. Learning what's
awry, finding what isn't
continuous in
                        the situations folks
get ourselves into, the shifts in setting, back-flashing, these shifts
in
diminishings across several hemispheres &
            next the Aelmihtig, treated
            like a God-damn moviegoer, is
given a high-end coffee table book about
                                        teeming
fungi. This sends the Divinity right back
to the incising board—*but that's not*
really me, nothing ever is I'm trying
I'm trying to tell you — look-it, it's

a bit sketchy but for starters there's
been a lot of illness in the Family, the one
real job is

to keep, is to keep, is to
avoid ending

up like your father

Stay with Me

1.

Not so easy to forget the puppet show of my past
lives. Might anyone have left some instructions

behind? What can that possibly mean, I ask
the child sitting in front and behind me.

There, there, she says. I'm a lot like you.
We've unskinned. The thermometer's

reached green. We can wait it out. You
keep saying that. I'm formless again. It's

O.K. Hold still. The laptop's decoding
cyber-colour and whispering karmic self-

pity for the second time. And no word of ours
has ever managed to escape. Not in the realm
of the possible. Not my line of mimicry.

2.

I need to let happening go. Meanwhile
a bottleneck event's under wraps. It's

O.K. Be beside yourself. Expiate. Do
you want to stay with us? We live

under real time. A verdict. Here's a
red ladder. It can be your superpower.

Undeterred by...

space trash spinning way upstairs in
the Low Earth orbit, today's newest

cloud is *pre*. Pre-oneiric. Pre-
historic. Is the colour
of stingray skin, is
mostly there
to reassemble
                    the evaporating water
ghosts, not the sky's dome-made-tangerine
from fires lost at sea. New as

a spray-on condom, and alone as a child
struggling to draw an octopus, the cloud's

a shambolic rehearsal, a violet
shroud with legacies
                    yet to learn—

What's loose, what's loose, what—

Increasingly Choreographed

Over Zoom. Looking across the lifeboat. None
of us can talk to our phones. Gone dead. How
should we narrate the unraveling life of you
scare me? If you feel you've been
here before then the child wants
to know where will
the rest of us live?
              The answer, it
turns out, is that a lot of people are
old and dying
habits.

    This gradually does not
help. Failings. The door-slamming
sublime, it's like
it knows—

Jubilate

1.
A voice told me, look you're here entirely because of me—

2.
Not always easy to overcome,

                      the origins of Collective Memory

can be traced back to the final

                      Bronze age, the Whitechapel

Fatberg and everything that helped

                      keep Jesus awake in church—

3.
Another voice said listen you don't

                      you still don't...it's not

these herds of digital dead people

                      people-watching it's not

the crowdfunded vigilantes: it's

                      that something...that original

astonishment that can't be walked

                      away from — the furies, the furies

            cross-pollinating

the wilderness inside bored toddlers

                      the moment in which the patient

remembers the mother-of-pearl cliffs of sunlight

                  asleep on a grandmother's
                  bathroom floor—

4.
Each of us an unlocked cabinet

of unfed mountain inside

the cage of ribs that sings so.

Sings so.

The New World of Not

What makes us feel liberated is not total freedom, but rather living in a set of limitations that we have created and prescribed for ourselves.

–Andrea Zittel

What Needs Saying

I hate this, he tells me,
my diminishing father
               unused
to living inside
this steady yet
             almost
imperceptible
encirclement—
          yet
cavernous
the secret space
between
the day-long
TV and where
he sits, remote
clutched
in hand—
         the wall
of nearby books may as well be knots of sun in the rain
         fraying
his brain cells often
overrule him   they're
decluttering one day, and the next
they've become a brazen
frontier he can't
comprehend
        the dormant = rioting
there—
      cast inside what's hurt what's tired beyond tiredness

Take a Path in the Snow

—after an image by Jeremy Stewart, *In Singing, He Sings a Song*

A path kids going to school have made
                                    between a chain link fence
and a scattering of evergreens—
                        Now photocopy it all
almost to death and what's real
                        creeps in. It does. Neither
more, nor less. I once saw a man
                                do this to each of our childhoods:
stood by the copying machine for
                        an afternoon in the hospital.

                Gliding. Carefully discarding

what can't be held. You could have installed
                                    an un-trashed subway inside
his fingers as they worked:
                        making visible what, without
him, might never
                have been found.

The Dark Barking

passing strange my
grandfather naked

smashing at the ice
to swim and save

a shower. Each
morning the mind's

intravenous infusion
of harmlessly

suspicious, chasing
forgetfulness and

where else is
there to go—

Good-looking
and very active

he writes on
a table cloth

unsettled with White
Owl cigar ash & pinched

with clothespins
the women keep

leaving behind. Keeps
explaining why

a few wrong
turns a man

can't help but
be a devourer

suspended inside
nothing is really

like me—

Is Also the Moment When

1.

Signs call from the scattershot
the precise tundra, its bare shoulders not
what apples once were for Cezanne. My face, my face
is locally sourced and scoured down, sewn together
by a do-it-yourself documentary: a life uneasily
is also

        the moment when. The riches of
winter they've gotten   they've—

2.

Can you actually become another woman?
A confusion of dead microphones rocking
gently round her feet, her skin burning bright
as yesterday's shiny little sins. Let's solicit

> What we call our life is nothing but a remnant, the odor of a fire that
> has been put out long ago...We live in a falsified world. The same words
> are repeated but they express nothing. In our language there is one
> truthful word only: chaos.
>   –Willem Frederik Hermans

some volunteers and livestream all of us
                                we're
scraps   we're what allows what matters
in addictions to listen in—

Can Anyone Stay Still

compos mentis you know?
                                    Shut up
and resurrect the old
xxxx, the old world gone
with it, banjaxed, it's the new
world of not. Here's
                         not here
and how I've forgotten how
to shop-lift safely and I can't
hear the high notes, they can't
muscle in no-more-no to tell
of the mystery—LOL—not

a single *harmonia mundi*
containing shelter-words
and cellular dynasties never
before seen and is life, life
is stranger-than-the-real
thing, an unlocked
before

and after, it's
no secret
the answer is
we didn't.

Hullaballoo Sign Repair

Poetry's privileged perch is not stable. "Poetry is speech by someone who is in trouble," is one poet's definition. There are more elegant definitions, but this one points to its primal aspect. Experience need not be assimilated. Art need not be separated. The poet would bid Virginia Woolf out of the Ouse emptying the stones from her pockets. She would that artists endure.

    –C.D. Wright, "The Book that Jane Wrote"

Ars Poetica

They asked me how long I'd been in
salvage-espionage and hullaballoo sign
repair. Take some time, I mean, give or
take, it's all in your head, right? Realism
beckons. All you need is

a laptop, a manipulative
childhood and a bag of sizzling
thunderclaps. A satisfactory
soundtrack. The talkative
and unraveling
brain's
            a baggage carousel. Decorative
tinder. An invasive plant called complicity. A
voice-over mentioning what remains
to be said isn't done much any
more. Afterthoughts of what
will have happened. And behind
which door did your lover learn to harness
nonstop hypnagogia? To be fair sometimes

people are ghost-mushrooms speaking
complex sentence patterns via electrical impulses
and other times a person is a peripatetic dog and a bicycle
wheel withdraws into a wilderness of teeth—

The Portable Mystic

An inflorescence of decades
that know how to pause, even
genuflect
        before
their time. Their single
chance: necessarily nominalist
and inimitable each
time. Un-gradual. It can't
be

but in their study of past-life
regressions, flowers
make
exhibitionists of us all—

Everybody, please fly south. No.
Inspect, even jettison
your thought
experiment, the one that's barely
one life-why long.
             Holding-her-self, animal-aging
sleep is more than merely
a distance. With an accruing
mean streak. To traditionalists, I say:

A dinner party should focus
on the main point. It's wise to

dwindle every now before
then. Advises an art critic newly
dead   oh shit, the microphone's
still
on. How have I never

noticed what's a cautionary tale
is a great
question and at least
it's still warm.

Stories are for Children

Yammers the lyric
ice pick with absolutely
zero fear
      of surrendering to
memories, meandering creatures
with no capacity
to mate for life. A breadline
roped in and waiting. The migrating
womb of the moral
                community, its agile
and disintegrating mind. Each day

an obituary, the psyche composed
of rivals and sends—a birthday party
trampoline, the mescaline flare
of smoked paprika in the wild, the pulse of
                unhurry
and the world to come, the world's soon-to-be
extinct
technique
of info-washing, its disavowal of
          endless
scarcity. Heat. Roped in
and what happened

    ◀▶

when things happen

Machines Can Learn

Bullseye	Baroque	Interlocutor
Original	Umbilical	Ambassador
Critizen	Cognitive Extension	Coruscates

Whatchaya looking at?   A glitch?   Machines can learn.

□

I would like to thank I want to
thank my hard-working Takumi
frying pan, the way it summons
blackening cliffs when
watching me from
afar. No, you

go first, insists the unhinged table for two, offering Gaboxadol
for my inside-out, time-saving, situational brain and making
that weird, fragile face it likes, a

                                        wraparound
emergency smile rippling
into this morning's do-it-yourself
N.F.T.

□

Assemblages are living, throbbing confederations that are able to function despite the persistent presence of energies that confound them from within. They have uneven topographies because...

 –Jane Bennett, *Vibrant Matter: A Political Ecology of Things*

Longevity. Duck fat ^{simmering.} Spark
plugs. Yaffle. Footfall. Admitting no
wrong-doing. Stainless, geological
linguistics. Nurdles. Are you
hearing correctly? Mindful
aquaculture. The colour red.
R.S.V.P. Homogeneous
substrate. Nothing's

□

foolproof—
      I don't find these words or even the ascetic spaces
dancing between very nourishing
                              objects
historical exactitude.

      Correctly, most people would
aver, adding: *Listen, you gotta keep it light, stick up*
for the less popular, provide an untrustworthy
non-sequitur when you can before
leaving the beset and hidebound streets
                   all behind. *And don't forget to let us know about*
                     your experience of the Northern Hake you
                     purchased at last year's steepening tailgate

party. Whatchaya looking
for? The Talented Mister? A solar flare? A faraway

□

bicycle made of childhood's perfectly imagined
static of snow? A headfirst collision with never's
equivalent? It's always a bit of a surprise, never
mind, but damn
                          if ethics doesn't inspire
queasy culinary conversations—
you just gotta work hard at sticking
around
the juddering humans juddering nearby

This Poem is the Human Equivalent (i)

Of an injured rubber spider. I would like
to make one of the words in this sentence
go away. I don't mean I want to replace
a word. I mean: make it disappear.

But words aren't easily scared off, each obeys
an ancient impulse to stay. The daily

...

spins, an immensity
of *I*, *you*, *we* all   ruthlessly, *they*
all socio-biologically, psychosexually crave—

> Aim for no delirium, nor
> animosity...and a few hours
> later a closing thunderstorm
> staring at the earth and a sadness
> that's acquisitive, kind of freaked
> out, lonely. Uncomfortable in my
> own skin, last night I found
> myself watching a crowded
> horror movie, only to realize
> at the end
> that I'd seen it before. Not

until the very end ← as for the frightening, they're
everywhere

This Poem is the Human Equivalent (ii)

of some
     worn tires, a
          classic snow globe, a Fitbit fetish. No, it's
               really the feral
umbrella growling   following me   I am behind
myself   I am lost I'm   lost I am   an edgeless obstacle
               gone astray—

Realia

I think the sense of the thinness of reality is where we are now,
because we're asking ourselves what other political arrangements
could come out of this situation? Could we end up in an
authoritarian state? Who has to be taken away to the camps for
it to start feeling real to ordinary people? The lesson from history
is that you can go all the way through without it feeling real.
You can be a good German and have the concentration camp
outside your town, and you can still not feel that's
something connected to you.
–Hari Kunzru

Growing Up the Only Children

of antler-clashing and the air we breathe,
world events make the most of brief
appearances. With no formal training

and kept drugged in a bunk bed for an eternity
or more, History's a misunderstood home
wrecker of flash-mob ingenuity. Originality.
Unsteady, sure, but I love living this way.
                              In dotage and
as kidnapped as any holy relic.

          But some good *has* come of the time
Jonah and Little Red Riding Hood were forced
to change places.
                    Hopelessly roaming, banging
on a can and then making the world's
largest database for rewilding
fragments and the need for
full-spectrum, microtonal
forgiveness. I can barely

hear them, either.
                    The next generation of
migratory birds is lured penniless by sound
pollution and then poisoned by sky
garbage in the unstoppered
                              and sacrificial
                                        the   inscrutable orphan-light

Awake to the Nearby

A colour-blind octopus
awake to the hybrid

nervous systems of nearby
materiality unspools

its skin to invent
                         an undulating
light show ⟶ orpiment orange
                                     ⟶ peppering
all the way to the blue
of a Verditer fly-
catcher ⟶ another turnstile flicker ⟶
                                     iridophores sift
into the mauve
of sleeping asparagus ⟶
                          then revamp the straw yellow
found on a polar bear's
oily coat ⟶ just in time for some bursts
of psilocybin jade. Intemperate

this poppy shimmer of meadow sprung
from triple-hearted fun   these lenticular
fireworks performing gratis
            ancient and impending this glee
a conjuring never needing to be seen

> Impaired hypoxia tolerance could reduce the possible dens usable
> by octopuses to only those well-ventilated dens or force octopuses
> out of dens entirely

nor followed by anyone

Realia (i)

This is old faux barbed-wire, taken from a ripped up movie set.
This device for capturing shade wasn't alive when you were born.
We live in a time when the Atlantic is diagnostically homeless.
They've lost their coping mechanism. Who can replace it? I'm with

you on leaving what's happening offers a psycho-pharmacologist:
violent-merciful present-oblivion industrial-woodlands. Trenchant
and unstoppable as a medical detective story. Of greater
consequence: an unexpectedly deliberate word that eludes sprawl
or capture—

People Eat Darkness

Generalizing about your own era is a mug's game, but...ours
is a jittery, in-between culture: allergic to the monumental,
skeptical of "greatness" (scare quotes mandatory), and
enthralled by aesthetic forms once thought minor.
—Jackson Arn

Do you have to have been born
into an imposter species
to commiserate with the true
crime addict?
      The adopted signature
of the doppelgänger means getting
hazard pay for that place we
keep losing in the head. Concealing
an impulse-control disorder, no genre ever
dies albeit genres die shrink-wrapped
all of the time. Sanitized: mutant. People eat darkness. Read
until the very end. Watch. But what's outside, what's on
the lam what's to hear in
                  the hadn't factored in things, the beast
                   clawing the brain things, the purity
                      of gruesome-there and
                         unravel-here things?
             Prefer molecules prefer chaos prefer

Real-life-combustible and nearly wrecked as shreds
of cold-summery lobster meat? OK. Each puzzle-blossom
finds the drain on the floor. The spectator also not present. Most likely
well-educated, well-spoken, not yet middle-aged, the story will indeed
fall off of the bone. Shrugs and covers its tracks. Something degrades.
Why don't we stay we can't really say of course. Gold leaf sprinkles.
Vans on highways. Being born all over the place
ends filling up an entire life—

Realia (ii)

In 2020, Netflix released *Lost Girls*, a true-crime drama based on *Lost Girls: An Unsolved American Mystery* written by Robert Kolker, a long-form journalist. The unsolved mystery was the Gilgo Beach serial killings on Long Island. Between 1996 and 2011, young women were murdered, their remains left near the water. The film's camera turns various moments into immaculate compositions of light and drenched colour. Subdued drama: occasions of. Only weeks ago, a suspect was apprehended. Only he knows what he thought upon reading the book and then watching the film starring Amy Ryan.

↔

Plumpes Denken. Crude thinking. 'The most important thing is to learn to think crudely. Crude thinking is the thinking of great men.'
Walter Benjamin paraphrasing Bertolt Brecht.

The moral responsibility of climate change is much murkier. Global warming isn't something that might happen, should several people make some profoundly shortsighted calculations; it is something that is already happening, everywhere and without anything like direct supervisors. Nuclear Armageddon, in theory, has a few dozen authors, climate catastrophe has billions of them...many of who eagerly bought in. And who in fact quite enjoy their present way of life. That includes, almost certainly, you and me and everyone else buying escapism with our Netflix subscription.

David Wallace-Wells, *The Uninhabitable Earth*

Inside Oceans Is: A Lyric Essay for Katherine Mansfield

The person who writes essayistically is the one who composes
as he experiments, who turns his object around, questions
it, feels it, tests it, reflects on it, who attacks it from different
sides and assembles what he sees in his mind's eye and
puts into words what the object allows one to see under the
conditions created in the course of writing.

–Theodor Adorno, citing Max Bense

Or,

[our perceptions are already] ringed round for each of us by
that thick wall of personality through which no voice has ever
pierced.

–Walter Pater

And,

To sense this world of waters known to the creatures of the sea
we must shed our human perceptions of length and breadth
and time and place, and enter vicariously into a universe of
all-pervading water.

–Rachel Carson

□

Possibly it never existed—

New drone footage shows the giddy essence of things
now requires insurance premiums to increase. By contrast

the stunted speech of ocean slavery proclaims
there's nowhere everywhere to

hide. I still...
                    ...buy fish. Careful, you've already begun

the memory test. The problem doesn't lie
with Chinese gliding frogs, or even the premodern

gift for imagining novel things. You need
to be debonair. You need to relive

yourself and, to be fair, a good
question is a wink of

memento mori why is it that   what
should you be   not looking at   but

doing and what really   really is
the boundary between them? Every

alive and incorporeal place
is jaw-dropping

and busting apart. The horror
of the cargo ship. A hungry

□

and furtive excess of
black bile has made
me.

Brief pause.

↔

And yet one has these 'glimpses,' before which all that one
has ever written (what has one written?)—all (yes, all) that
one has ever read, pales [...] The waves, as I drove home this
afternoon, and the high foam, how it was suspended in the
air before it fell [...] What is it that happens in that moment
of suspension? It is timeless. In that moment (what *do* I
mean?) the whole life of the soul is contained. One is flung
up—out of life—one is 'held,' and then—down, bright,
broken, glittering on to the rocks, tossed back, part of the
ebb and flow.

February 1920, K.M., *Journal of Katherine Mansfield*

First, Chekhov.

You searched through stains
left on paper—Chekhov's diaries, his letters
torn from their former lives—all those
abandoned breaths in a room darkening
green with evening's elms, the light of a world
infinitely and progressively missing, you looked
and looked with his, your greedier eye, but
couldn't find him, couldn't
                              glimpse the wet bulk of his days, their chunks
of inconsequence—milky smooth animals
hanging skinned in
obscure abattoirs. And then
you wanted to toss everything
away except the stories.

Tonight I'm holding your journal, the one your husband
got published in 1927, this very book almost
one hundred years old, this book sprung
from a century
                    I can barely
touch, though the twentieth century made
its way into you with that telegram: your
brother lost in France (in what we came to call
the First World War), his remaining
words in France, *Lift my head, Katie, I can't
breathe.* And then you vowed
your sentences would be debts
sent to the dead.

□

You call yourself K.M. in these pages you never saw in print, these
small paragraphs that strip me, their brown eyes alive to
the spaces the world makes
around things. K.M. did you
                    smell me just beyond
the pale wilds of your skin, its blank
heat (as you once believed you could
find your missing brother)? It's not
a brother's love I'm offering. Meet me, not

in these words, nor in the sea's
high foam but in what's suspended
between them, meet
me here, caught between words
and foam.

You must now remember—

learning with your hands, those
pressed knees, either there's nothing worth keeping, or nothing
that can be kept, our lives don't
happen within us
that way.
            But I want
to tell you that tonight it's so utterly
cold the Saskatchewan wind can freeze the skin on your face
in less than a minute, a wind that sounds like workmen
taking axes to ice.

□

I want to remember how the light fades from a room—and
one fades with it, is *expunged*, sitting still, knees together,
hands in pockets.
–K.M. January 1, 1922

Only you have found this room, this everlasting
ever-emptying room the night settles over us, settles down
across us each day, pressing ocean thick
beneath our eyelids. And now you
must remember what you could never know, dying at
a naked 34—you can't ever become sufficiently
brutal to time and the many selves
time urges upon us. Would you marry me
I once asked you KM (as you liked to
call yourself), the moment I first finished
your garden party. The first of many
times. My amazed joy. You
looked away. Let me try something
else, throw in
        a children's library, a wide open
doorway that lets the sea and sand in, some
intimate apparel to reach into the space
beside you. No? Let me then go full
throttle: here's Tolstoy sipping, no
gulping from a sin-dappled glass
of dragonflies and maybe, maybe now
you'll make up your mind. Mirror
some neurons? No, she
says, I won't even
let you kiss me.

□

Naturally it's never enough
to cough up memories

about this stuff. Or mope. The universe
seems oddly framed, spews eons
of disregard into the atmosphere daily
and corners the market on our

feral comings and goings. I don't know how know
how to stay in the room
with this Thing—

A fact: a freestanding cylindrical aquarium holding about 1,500
exotic fish burst in Berlin this morning, causing a wave of
devastation in and around the tourist attraction. 1 million litres of
water poured out of the 14 metre-high tank shortly before 6: a.m.
None of the animals inside the salt-water aquarium, which contained
clownfish, teria batfish and palette surgeonfish, survived. One
witness feared a bomb had exploded. Berlin's mayor visited the scene
and remarked: "A proper tsunami poured forth over the premises of
the hotel and adjacent restaurants. If the whole thing had happened
an hour later, we would have had to report terrible human damage."
Emergency services shut down the major road that leads from
Alexanderplatz toward the Brandenburg Gate owing to the large
volume of water. Material fatigue was the likeliest cause behind the
accident. Very few tourists were nearby when a torch-lit parade of
hundreds of thousands went through the Brandenburg Gate toward
Unter den Linden on April 20, 1939 to celebrate Hitler's 50th birthday.
Although I didn't visit the aquarium when I was in Berlin a few
weeks ago, I passed through this district on my way to the National
Gallery to see Caspar David Friedrich's painting *Monk by the Sea*.

□

A political fable: a freestanding cylindrical aquarium holding about 1,500 exotic fish burst in Berlin this morning, causing a wave of devastation in and around the tourist attraction. 1 million litres of water poured out of the 14 metre high tank shortly before 6: a.m. None of the animals inside the salt-water aquarium, which contained clownfish, teria batfish and palette surgeonfish, survived. One witness feared a bomb had exploded. Berlin's mayor visited the scene and remarked: "A proper tsunami poured forth over the premises of the hotel and adjacent restaurants. If the whole thing had happened an hour later, we would have had to report terrible human damage." Emergency services shut down the major road that leads from Alexanderplatz toward the Brandenburg Gate owing to the large volume of water. Material fatigue was the likeliest cause behind the accident. Very few tourists were nearby when a torch-lit parade of hundreds of thousands went through the Brandenburg Gate toward Unter den Linden on April 20, 1939 to celebrate Hitler's 50th birthday.

□

A miserable day. In the night I thought for hours of the evil
of uprooting. Every time one leaves anywhere, something
precious, which ought not to be killed, is left to die.
    –K.M. February 9, 1922

It astonished you how a house made
of words is always
better than anything we
can be or forget or say: a house
made of words lifts, flings
us away from our times. And yet
without your rage, your quicksilver delights, and anarchy, your
vigilance, no words can happen, pool
beneath each other, each story
of yours saying
            No
each story saying
            No
once again to the long betrayal, each story

the encounter between faces, and still, even now, no one
knows for whom stories
are told.

You must now remember—

    Inside oceans is

        Poetry an artifact of the world that has ended.
        Michael Robbins, "A Conversation About Trees"

a different place
now—

It's a weird time, Quinn said

> [speaking of] the pandemic era. People are saying weird
> shit because there's almost nothing *to* say and there are no
> solutions.
> —Colin Quinn

1.

Elizabeth Barrett Browning once gave the poetry of her husband,
Robert's poetry, a harsh assessment, criticizing his habit of
excessively paring down his syntax with opaque results. "You
sometimes make a dust, a dark dust," she wrote him, "by sweeping
away your little words."

2.

To support myself, to pay for things, for most of forty years I've
explained away what didn't work, doesn't, never did, indeed can
cause serious side effects. As suddenly no one had any.

What this all adds up to is that two wrongs do make a right is what
keeps slasher-porn movies in business.

3.
Tumbledown. Underneath my sight underneath the
rime ice, beneath me beneath every
thing is
that tenderer alter-
life. Whatever can these
                              lively
reminders mean? Singing by eye, Listen: don't
just translate
an autograph: do
things, do something resembling
normal life   which means please talk
me out of it, it's starting

the self-inflicted creature's thinking
is on other things: Listen, some people they

do whatever they want
to get lulz—

Usually When

foreign material is transplanted into tissue, be it on Sunday or
inside the epipelagic zone a kind of crime has already...

Everyone knows our varying strengths require competing
nude selfies and we're not at all in this together...

Long believed lost forever, A.I. is honestly sorry to bother
viewers, but how do you care for wintry truth-telling...

When even the oldest are still a talent to watch after all
                    these predatory

years, each of everybody is
a recovering childhood addict—

There's been a Murmur in My Head

Both phobic anxiety and obsessive-compulsive disorders concern behavior that is, objectively speaking, at odds with a sense of self. The obsessive and compulsive drive, which can motivate a subject to expend his or her energy on a series of Sisyphean tasks...only appear meaningless if we subtract these acts from a broader context. The precise manifestation is less important than the need to localize the vortex of anxiety, which, in the absence of the obsessive act, emerges as an all-consuming, violent force that threatens to destroy the subject.

–Dylan Trigg, *Topophobia: A Phenomenology of Anxiety*

Despite Limited Life Experience

the journey is made almost alone. A raga spun
from the umbilical cord—a telescope
composed of □ sheets of
disintegrating time. A placenta
whose travails are contemplated
by the interactive evolution of pigment
sprinkled across the egg of a heron, a long sliver
of hectic genealogy + screen memories ⟶ these melancholy

notations the result of brain shrink
and the agoraphobic
peregrinations of the heart: it's untenable
this toothless struggle to reach
the bottom of the food chain, a target
with room inside
for everyone, these
        days lifted from the glossy = the quick and dirty
the bodily fluids of the ephemeral, its torrential
everything
        stripped down,
and botched
to the core ⟵

There's been a Murmur

in my head for as long as I can remember—

*

Ordinary objects—a keepsake river stone on the window ledge, my phone on the table—openly request that I position them in the way most suitable to their temperaments. They desire to be placed just so—

Something bad will happen if I don't cross a patio or wash dishes the right way. An endless patter of instructions. To avoid disaster, a voice indicates the correct bunch of asparagus I must buy in the grocery store. Dozens of times each day I'm urged to perform an action or say a certain word to protect my children from harm.[4]

*

Part of having OCD means that certain people (not everyone) can listen in on my thoughts. They can be standing still nearby—waiting for an elevator, say—but I can sense them moving about inside my mind. A few others have amused themselves with my memories.

*

Words are objects. They have multiple dimensions on the screen, in my mind, and on a page in a book. Each with its own personality, a core that persists over time. Very few are noisy. Many slightly resent

---

4 In *The Man Who Couldn't Stop: OCD and the True Story of a Life Lost in Thought*, David Adam cites a speech made by MP Charles Walker to the British House of Commons in 2012: "One is constantly making deals with oneself...I was on holiday recently and I took a beautiful photograph of my son carrying a fishing rod. There was my beautiful son carrying a fishing rod, I was glowing with pride and then the voice started, `If you don't get rid of the photograph, your child will die'" (246). I receive similar commands many times each day. Walker's internal commands match my own.

being combined with other words. *Intrinsic* and *falling* choose this category. Also *immerse*. The word *loot* however, craves company.

*

Very often I suddenly perceive memories of events and images that don't belong. They're entirely alien. An unexpected noise—sharp and brittle—can cause those memories to flare across my mind's eye. A sailing cutter ship on ocean whitecaps. A lacquer cabinet in an airy room at dusk.

My life seems inexplicably porous.

*

One winter almost twenty years ago when I needed to take cabs home at night, I got to know many of the local drivers. Once a new one picked me up and after only a few seconds he realized that I'd sensed he was a serial killer that no one knew about. We drove along like that, him smug, enjoying how I was becoming increasingly agitated until I asked him to stop the car and let me out. But we're not at your destination, he protested, speaking very, very serenely. Now, please, *stop* the car, I shouted and he pulled over on the expressway. When I picture him now, I can see his almost round face, Derby hat, narrow black tie, and white shirt. Hear his very slight English accent. I knew he was just passing through and driving a taxi to make some money. He said nothing as I left the cab, but he made it clear that I amused him and that he was extending leniency—

*

There's a moment in *The Godfather,* Part 3, when Al Pacino-Michael Corleone, an aging Mafia Don and diabetic, collapses with a sudden decline in his glucose. He'd just confessed to a priest that he had his brother murdered, and the priest offered that the body responds to mental anguish. Watching this scene a few weeks ago, I felt my system flood with cortisol. With no desire nor intention to do so, I absorb other people's emotions.

Earlier this year, I sent an email to a friend on her birthday. She replied within an hour of my note, letting me know that she'd become homeless and was living in her car. We spoke on the phone, her voice wavering between an almost normal conversational tone and stuttering panic. It isn't for me to tell her story, but so many of the awful things that can happen to a person have been inflicted on her. We've spoken often in the meantime and almost always my body reacts instantly. Although I'm not diabetic, my glucose sometimes plummets and I have to eat something. Or acid reflux begins to sear through my chest, making it feel as though my upper body is on fire.

My sternum and lungs can burn like that for days. I envision threads of lava.

It's like I'm a sponge for her grief. And I can't control it, hard as I try. After one conversation with her, I had to lie in bed for almost two hours silent and entirely motionless. I'm not saying that I'm a good person for reacting to the pain of other people this way; in fact, it has nothing to do with ethics or conscious imagination; it just happens and I wish it wouldn't. I can't help thinking, though, that this sort of porous membrane I live amidst must influence so many things in my response to the world. I can't know how much freedom I can exercise in who I am. But there are good things: is this lack of a protective layer what makes me drawn to colour? A Rothko painting can push so deeply into the psyche that it eradicates everything except itself. The orange-red eyes of oystercatchers on the coast are sentient buttons that seem to arrive from the future.

*

A red comes from its own past, responding not to our question but to its own, seeking its redness beyond the moment and elsewhere.

–Alphonso Lingis, *The Imperative*

I've torn a photograph from a magazine showing colour tests the painter Pat Steir made for her Manhattan studio and hung it on a window frame in this room. Numerous lines of paint drip down like a beaded curtain—multiple shades of plum blue that Steir seems to favour (I'm thinking of her *Winter Daylight*), some yellow and a dull green. It's the matte red, though, that I keep returning to because it's the closest match I've found to the dark chevron on a male rose-breasted grosbeak I saw in the spring.

Most male grosbeaks have fuchsia triangles on their white chests, so I wondered how female grosbeaks felt about this one, with its darker feathers, somewhere between arterial red and smoked paprika. Because it was mid-May, the foliage of the poplars hadn't grown in and I was able to peer up at the bird for fifteen or twenty minutes as it preened, moved from branch to branch, perched. Even when the bird flew elsewhere, the red has remained with me. During those moments in the forest, the intrusive (and yet whimsical) voices that continually command me to carry out their will disappeared. They've since returned—as I knew they would—and I've tried hard to take Steir's colour tests within myself as an antidote to their poison, but to no avail.

Though these voices would bristle at the word *poison*. They would say that they're helping me avoid calamity. Perhaps though, the situation is even more complex. Marcel Proust would possibly theorize that these voices act to shield me from the fear of danger, rather than danger itself.[5] That is, part of my psyche is attempting to protect itself from acknowledging the precarious nature of reality: to face, in fact, one's powerlessness might risk a breakdown. My sense is, however, that these voices are not allies: they rarely let up. To offer a physiological comparison, their continual demands are similar to having a system deranged by too much caffeine. Except that a coffee buzz goes away, whereas the voices and their attendant anxiety stay: someone with OCD is both adrift and stalled in their ongoing distress.

*

Colour dazzles, especially when it emanates from a living creature; it seems to be something continuously new, permanently beautiful. Colours are mysterious, half concealing something, though what's there is present in plain sight. Colours stay the way they're born, existing apart from where we find them. As Kandinsky claims, "the glow of red is within itself." The red-billed oxpecker grooms its favourite antelope for ticks; the rush of hemoglobin passing between three matter-of-fact creatures—bird, arthropod, mammal—retains the same colour when exposed to air. As Wittgenstein puts it, "something red can be destroyed, but red cannot be destroyed...it makes no sense to say that the colour red is torn up or pounded to bits." Even so, the situation we meet with

---

5 See *In Search of Lost Time*, Volume II *Within a Budding Grove*, 252.

colours is hard to understand. If different cultures and historical periods respond to colours variously,[6] there is a sense that colour itself provides an alternative, even an antidote to history. Immediately upon starting Toni Morrison's *Beloved*, the reader encounters Baby Suggs, a woman whose "past had been like her present—intolerable—and since she knew death was anything but forgetfulness, she used the little energy left her for pondering color." She initially sets her sights on lavender, but as the book progresses, we learn that "she had exhausted blue and was well on her way to yellow." Put differently, the reflections of the setting sun in the photograph below are an unmediated, actual orange-red, though the sun is only an image. If people today worry about the duplicity of digital life, we rarely consider how a colour is one phenomenon that persists whether on a bird in a forest or a mechanically-reproduced image.

*

Friday is family movie night, but Saturday is when my wife and

6 For a wide-ranging historical survey of the colours in Western culture see Michel Pastoureau's fascinating accounts of red, blue, yellow, green and black.

I choose a movie for ourselves or spend some time with a TV series, most of which don't retain our interest long enough to watch every season. Lately, it has been *Russian Doll*, recommended by an old friend (a man who fronts his own band, and is one of the smartest and most relentlessly unhappy people I know). The series concerns a woman, Nadia, who repeatedly dies and returns to her ongoing life and then dies again, all amidst a rainy, TV-New York City-as-Bardo-scape. We'll probably see the show to the end. One Saturday, though, only a little while after seeing the grosbeak in the poplar forest, we deferred turning on the TV to go for a walk around the man-made lake not far from where we live. Waiting for me beneath an overpass while I scanned the lake for recently migrated shorebirds, my wife saw a battered pigeon lying in the dirt.

The bird had likely been struck by a car, and it had been there for some time. Its legs struck out 180 degrees to its body, but it was still alive. It blinked as ants walked over its face, pooled in its eyes. I found a tree branch the width of a broom handle, placed it over the bird's neck, stepped on both sides of the branch, rocked back and forth until I'd killed the creature. Its lavender-pink tongue protruded, slightly vibrated as I pushed down.

We had nothing in which to dispose of the body and so we left it on the gravel incline. Two days later I passed by the same place to find the corpse missing its head and much of its upper chest. The flesh had been picked clean to the vertebrae but most of the bird was intact. The following day everything was gone.

I don't know what it means to perpetuate things in words, whether these words refer to the atrociously wounded pigeon or the unfortunate association I couldn't help making—and couldn't erase—when I was killing the bird. Numerous survivors from the

Nazi camps tell of how Kapos would often murder an inmate by taking a shovel, placing it on the inmate's throat and rocking back and forth until the person died.[7]

*

"Every living situation," observes Jonathan Crary, "has a new face that has never been and will never come again." The dying pigeon looked at me and if its face seemed to emanate that it understood *what* I was doing to it, the creature couldn't have discerned *why* I was causing it such pain.

I couldn't bear to see ants scurrying over its face, dipping into its open eyes.

If I remarked earlier that colours have an existence apart from their specific embodiments—the unalterable red of the grosbeak's chevron and the Steir colour test are the same—and that it makes sense that Morrison offers her character a respite from her appalling life by granting her the capacity to fix her mind on various colours, I didn't anticipate that the words *pink* and *lavender* in her novel would merge with the colours of the pigeon's flushed tongue. A colour can't be destroyed, but to meet the shining pink and petal-soft lavender was to encounter not only misery, but what Simone Weil calls "affliction":

Human thought is unable to acknowledge the reality of affliction. To acknowledge the reality of affliction means saying to oneself:

---

7 Michael André Bernstein points to the "prevalent danger that haunts readers of literature on the Shoah: that of becoming so caught up in the material that, compared with its intensities, other themes, ideas, and emotions seem insignificant." I agree with his position in general terms (to view a contemporary freight train as one "'crammed with suffocating children'" is misguided and possibly perverse), but having to kill a creature in this manner, something I'd only encountered in my reading about the camps, made the comparison impossible to avoid.

'I may lose at any moment, through the play of circumstances over which I have no control, anything whatsoever that I possess, including those things which are so intimately mine that I consider them as being myself. There is nothing I might not lose. It could happen at any moment that what I am might be abolished and replaced by anything whatsoever of the filthiest and most contemptible sort.'

—Simone Weil, "Human Personality"

*

I suspect that most people with OCD comprehend in varying degrees how our behaviour is a kind of ineffectual talisman meant to ward off chaos and potential calamities; and I further imagine that we resent the voices that direct us to navigate fear in such debilitating ways. I can't speak for others, but I've found that the most effective way to step outside the enclosure OCD sequesters me inside, is to accept a kind of rudimentary nihilism. There's no point in attempting to manipulate reality because creatures such as ourselves are entirely of no importance. We are entirely subject to contingency because the world...

*

...is chaos. A bird can lie in agony until someone comes along to kill it or not; earlier that day it could move its body to intertwine itself in weaving patterns in the air with the rest of its flock and then all of that perhaps joyful activity stopped. I wish that I could say that this understanding nullifies the voices in my mind that instruct me to write the word *ventricle* right now, but it hasn't. Next: *feldspar.* The disease keeps me in a perpetual state of childhood: aware of the precarious, I'm fussy, insipidly self-absorbed and easily upset. Compared to many, my life is a safe and well-padded one and yet, each day's a glitch, and I know what it's like to feel instant chagrin upon coming to in an ICU. I think a good word to use is *stupid*; it's unbelievably stupid to live like this. More than fifty years ago, I had to do things in pairs: wash my hands, and then touch the hot and cold faucets one after the other, once, twice. But something inside would tell me that I wasn't doing it right, so I needed to start over. As a teenager, I learned that a case-cutter from my job at the grocery store could release me from having to do things in pairs but I haven't done something like that since my twenties.

ventricle   feldspar   ventricle.

To communicate with strangers—

*

Do you feel as though today is today?   I never know how.

Black Fire

the mentally ill
                        each

a black fire; those near
them—children,
spouse—other

                        people's
days not
even ash

I Can't Remember What I Came Here to

The autotropic world interior (universal capitalism) [is] a
self-determining and so self-terminating world, one in which
extinction—self-extinction—is in vogue and something we
will pay to see.
   –Mark Seltzer, *The Official World*

Surveillance is Autobiography (i)

Microphones
made of minutes
                        crowding
the shower stall are
logging the one-way
excursion of this naked
meat puppet aging
within and without

                        breathing particulates
of anxiety decades deep   memory as presentiment
of attack and decay the cottony loss so deep
it requires sutures and patience shrugs
its shoulders...hey, it's time

to wake up half-on the grass and
half-on the sidewalk everyone taller
than a Barbie waving a greeting
already beginning to disappear

these increments of days these
irrevocable bystanders overhearing
the mind humming
along
a scene   from *Macbeth*
in its jaw-clenching
                        chary
brain pan

—

Surveillance is Autobiography (ii)

Question: would you have your tattoo preserved
and turned into the cover protecting your future's
very own hand-held autobiographical novel?

                                      Anthropodermic
Bibliopegy becoming the newest thing among
the counter-history crowd. (Peptide mass fingerprinting
even working with what's left of whales.) Look

                                            you gotta replace
traditional contemplation with newfangled
confrontation, change your mind and ask
yourself how much of the bystander effect
we should extend to ourselves. Smart

phones are traumatized by what's popped
into their mouths and ears. Their brains. Errant, eternally
circulating eye sockets. Not so [private] guess-work
toggling with scenes of forgotten guilt displaying
mysterious sub-puritanical symptoms. Listen
                                 in: the purpose
of the jitters is to cry
out
   to philosophy *when
did surprise actually
begin its begin?* Dammit. This viral thing's endlessly
                              hexed and efflorescent green the colour
of a filter-bubble made of a million lost honeycreeper
wings. A spreadsheet made of minutes
and chronic air-lift fatigue mean
I'm not making any of this up and I never
did play Pavlovian chess, nor even
air guitar, and I never could

figure out
prerequisite school—

But I do have tantrums.

Don't You Know Where You Belong?

Imagine if we did. Like sound people everywhere,
the mind's maintenance crew is working on habits
alive since the Middle Ages and betting on the self-
taught arsonist who performs to birdsong and
keeps showing up in this beautiful second-hand home.

Invariably, Seagulls

Who would have guessed that, on retiring, Constantinople would be
given a blue leather briefcase decorated with gold-leaf and inside

it a Koran and an iPhone showing Yeats on a scavenger hunt?
No answer.
        Instead, this:

  —Seagulls, like most humans and most other creatures, spend
most of their time doing nothing, just standing there. You could
call this a form of waiting. To stand in this world waiting: for the
next meal, for death, for sleep. I don't know how they die.
        Orhan Pamuk, "Seagull in the Rain"

Look I agree with you   ↔   but why should you be spared?

I Can't Remember What I Came Here to

say. I write this with the hand of a mannequin I found
rigid beneath an air mattress
                                        the ordinary rubbery kind like
those emergency shoes someone tosses into
the thinking
closet. Today

    each word is a guest

visiting alongside the crime
writer from ancient
oddball Amsterdam
                                        the same one
who showed
me Zen. Inside this canal-
cave
of a sentence weathers
this scarecrow warmed

by bewilderment and wearing
a gasmask for a hat
                                        she keeps telling me
what's gift-wrapping and what's
makeshift
discarnate *hello* / *hello* and
every word is part

ndered squandered squandered squandered squandered squandered squandered squandered squandered squandered squandered squandered

of the inaudible, the disruptive
      present
except when it is not—

But if vice in a human is the same Thing as poor vision in an owl

how can the creatures of this earth imagine ever-restless
humanity? The genes for superbugs waiting in Norway's arctic and
the aging mind of the man threatening to go on a hunger strike
unless he gets more sophisticated video games. Anders Behring
Brievik imprisoned for life for mass murder and how should you
cope with what anthropologists suspect may be the
conundrum

of the co-discovered
and unrepentant
material world?

Its *hush...*
We must

2.
... traffic in the contours of those profligate
picoseconds that ghost-write colour
to our open and sleep-steady brains: we
must traffic in garage rock going toe-to-toe
with perceiving something in its entirety
in the psych ward I spent a week in downtown. Its

hush.

3.

And the unavoidable descendant, unable to listen, keeps practicing
a farewell speech, keeps reading it aloud to a long pile
of dirt stretched out like an afternoon in
a drunken lawn chair. Oblivion's
physically demanding, but what's invisible in your sleeping
bag is one way to repay that debt to nature. Got

your back, I promise
blares soothing magenta (Martin Senour Roman Violet No. 2225)—

Serious Stories

When I was young, serious stories always had someone
raking and burning leaves and the leaves were stealing
gin, often from vampires heading off to join yesterday's
barely perceptible war just in time

> (A generation that had gone to school on a horse-drawn streetcar now stood under
> the open sky in a countryside in which nothing remained unchanged but
> the clouds, and beneath these clouds, in a field
> of force of destructive torrents
> and explosions was the tiny, fragile human body.
>
> Walter Benjamin, "The Storyteller")

for a new decade to intercept what's fastened
beneath the old one. Televisions were made
from our mother's laps and cactus in a riparian
setting mostly animals loved; and some people

expected picnics, plus the exacting ambivalence of nothing
entirely going on. Others were promised their children's
eventual release, that time would be a rip cord
of sorts. And these faces were commonly
placed on rare sheets of corrugated film that dwarf
light softens, quotes and then scrubs free ←→

But WTF...

Netizens, speak to me: how is it we're not beside ourselves by what
we've done, what we've —→

ians make mistakes make humans mistakes make humans biosensors make mistakes make incentives

wrought once upon this ipso facto ghosted
postmortem birthday app
these predatory and perpetually archived facial
cloud data maps = this permanently precarious world

= this self-tracking Pandora telematics prophet world
= this entirely staring multi-sharing world hypervigilant without end

←

We Need to Talk

1.
Life committing to any one thing. Heedless.
Urgencies. Lend us an improper state
of mind. A taking of sides, the grief-stricken
brush-and-ink painting shushing
somebody's partially-erased
information-saturated childhood. Marcel Duchamp sacrificed

2.

doll-size butterflies alive in winter
and gave me up
to his Virgil. *How* do you
know me again? Don't
leave home without
taking my life in
the pluperfect grip
of your hands. Has anyone gone
too far is no longer
an option. Splicing
terrifically. A laser if it's yours
to give. Old and in un-
forsaken love.

    A propensity for. In recognition
of. Virtue-signaling. Sweet-and-sour the everyday
premonition   IRL

3.

The maudlin streak-of-genius in
getting-to-know-you games
at work. The flash mob, I never have time
for. Admittedly the afternoon snow here
is sharp-shinned, streaked white   rusty
and is also using again. They're fed
the fairy tales, fed up, I mean. Is stockpile
a verb or
                a symptom? Whatcha gonna do
with your square of soil
                                your few spoonfuls
of nasty
historical fact the end coming
too soon is mostly some testy
philosophical cardboard. A tug, a pull
on the Jamesian tab. A coming-of-age story if
there only was one. You have
to figure out what's bird-

4.
less in cages. The archive. I think
I found what's so what's so
                    lovely, so
beautifully, in fact. Then one
of the Magi's getting a robocall
informing him that he, himself, is
the Anointed
One. But is anything beyond
working? It's pretty much
all-or-nothing. The shark on

fire's ghost-banishing Symbolist daydreams
of forced labour, no one can think for one solid
week after the say-so field surgery. It really is it really
is unaccountably wonderful to be a magnet and impossible
to believe oh man the infection the infectious
possibilities—

Abbr

turns out our migratory our
                       eventually
vagabond
        Life can't
go anywhere; the mind its very
own hospice or Quonset hut—

Notes

When Eyelids

For the Kleist citation, see https://en.wikipedia.org/wiki/The_Monk_ by_the_Sea.

For the Brentano citation, see Johannes Grave," *Caspar David Friedrich*, Prestel, 2012. The Griselda Pollock essay, "Photographing Atrocity: Becoming Iconic?" is in *Picturing Atrocity: Photography in Crisis.*

What is

Ivy Knight mentions that Arnold Schwarzenegger is a fan of the Stoics in "Reboot Dept. Stoic or Bust." *The New Yorker.* January 31, 2022. According to *Harper's Magazine* "Findings," February 2022, "Dutch and Japanese speakers can tell whether someone is laughing in Dutch or Japanese." The line "Genres / vivify / a need for which no alternative method exists" is a quiet riff off Michael McKeon's claim that "Genres fill a need for which no alternative method exists" in *The Origins of the English Novel.*

Undeterred by...

The notion of the "spray-on condoms" is Jan Vinzens Krause's, and is mentioned in the *Year in Ideas 2008, The New York Times Magazine.*

Take a Path in the Snow

The final lines are a version of Robert Bresson's remark "Make visible what, without you, might perhaps never have been seen" (cited by Geoff Dyer in *Zona: A Book About a Film About a Journey to a Room.)*

The Dark Barking

The phrase "chasing forgetfulness" is from Albert Camus' *The Myth of Sisyphus.*

Is Also the Moment When
The citation from Willem Frederik Hermans is from *Dutch Master: On Frederik Willem Hermans*. Rev. by Francine Prose. *Harper's Magazine*. July 2022.

Growing Up the Only Children
The information about migratory birds is a slight alteration of the following: "Migratory birds lured by light pollution are then poisoned by air pollution." "Findings." *Harper's Magazine*. January 2023.

Ars Poetica
The information referring to mushrooms using electrical impulses to form "complex sentence patterns" comes from "Findings," *Harper's Magazine*, July 2022, 80.

Awake to the Nearby
The lines referring to a colour-blind octopus inventing "a light show with its skin" come from Alphonso Lingis, cited by Elizabeth Grosz in *Chaos, Territory, Art: Deleuze and the Framing of the Earth*. The study that describes the damage that the rise in ocean acidification on octopuses may be found in: ttps://www.journals.uchicago.edu/doi/10.1086/712207

Realia
The photograph in this poem was taken at Ravensbrück (the Nazi concentration camp created specifically for women) in the fall of 2022. The train tracks were used by Siemens to transport material made by slave labourers.

Invariably, Seagulls
The question "but why should you be spared?" has a passage from Lauren Berlant's *Cruel Optimism* in mind: "Yet Muriel's question haunts: *Why should you be spared?* Muriel refers to aging and death, and to the slow decline of becoming sexually undesirable" (222).

People Eat Darkness
The phrase "people eat darkness" refers to Richard Lloyd Parry's *People Who Eat Darkness.*

Inside Oceans: A Lyric Essay for Katherine Mansfield
The information about the collapsed aquarium in Berlin can be found here: https://www.theguardian.com/world/2022/dec/16/huge-cylindrical-aquarium-housing-1500-exotic-fish-bursts-in-berlin

Elizabeth Barrett Browning Once
The quotation from Colin Quinn is from "Colin Quinn Just Wants to Make Small Talk," *The New Yorker.* January 30, 2023. The quotation from Elizabeth Barrett Browning comes from Ben Zimmer's "Crash Blossoms," *The New York Times Magazine,* January 21, 2010.

There's been a Murmur
For quotations from Bernstein, Crary, Kandinsky and Wittgenstein, see respectively: *Foregone Conclusions: Against Apocalyptic History; Scorched Earth: Beyond the Digital Age to a Post-Capitalist World; Concerning the Spiritual in Art; Philosophical Investigations.*

Surveillance is Autobiography (ii)
The information pertaining to "anthropodermic bibliopegy" and "peptide mass fingerprinting" comes from Mike Jay's review of Megan Rosenbloom's *Dark Archives: A Librarian's Investigation into the Science and History of Books Bound in Human Skin. The New York Review of Books.* November 5, 2020. The phrase "traditional contemplation with newfangled confrontation" (referring to Donald Judd's minimalist sculpture) is Peter Schjeldahl's.

But if vice in a human is the same Thing as poor vision in an owl
The comparison of vice in a human to poor vision in an owl comes
from "Philippa Foot: Telling Right from Wrong." James Ryerson, *New
York Times Magazine*, December 26, 2010: 42. Martin Senour Roman
Violet No. 2225 is the colour first used on signs indicating dangerous
radiation.

General Bibliography

Adam, David. *The Man Who Couldn't Stop: OCD and the True Story of a Life Lost in Thought*. Picador, 2014.

Berlant, Lauren. *On the Inconvenience of Other People*. Duke UP, 2022.

Bernstein, Michael André. *Foregone Conclusions: Against Apocalyptic History*. U of California P, 1994.

Crary, Jonathan. *Scorched Earth: Beyond the Digital Age to a Post-Capitalist World*. Verso, 2022.

Dyer, Geoff. *Zona: A Book about a Film about a Journey to a Room*. Vintage, 2012.

Grave, Johannes. *Caspar David Friedrich*, Prestel, 2012.

Kleist, Heinrich von. https://en.wikipedia.org/wiki/The_Monk_by_the_Sea

Lingis, Alphonso. *The Imperative*. Indiana UP, 1998.

Mansfield, Katherine. *Journal of Katherine Mansfield*. Ed. J. Middleton Murray. Constable, 1927.

Morrison, Toni. *Beloved*. New American Library. 1987.

Pollock, Griselda. "Photographing Atrocity: Becoming Iconic?" *Picturing Atrocity: Photography in Crisis*. Eds. Geoffrey Batchen and others. Reaktion Books, 2012.

Proust, Marcel. *In Search of Lost Time*. Vol. II. Trans. D.J. Enright and others. The Modern Library, 2003.

Trigg, Dylan. *Topophobia: A Phenomenology of Anxiety*. Bloomsbury, 2017.

Wallace-Wells, David. *The Uninhabitable Earth: Life After Warming*. Tim Duggin Books, 2019.

Weil, Simone. *An Anthology*. Trans. Richard Rees. Penguin, 2005.

Wittgenstein, Ludwig. *Philosophical Investigations*. Trans. G.E.M. Anscombe. Basil Blackwell, 1963.

Acknowledgments

This collection has been composed over some difficult years. Without the ongoing support of Amy Snider, my partner, and my children, Andy, Jesse and Jakob, I wouldn't have been able to complete the book. These poems and mini-essay are dedicated to them. And I further dedicate the book to birds everywhere.

Additionally, I've been grateful to have the support of many friends. Thank you Philip Charrier, a colleague and friend who has always offered support. A single conversation with him substantially altered the way I write. His brilliant photography inspires all of my work. Susan Lohafer, likely the most gifted reader I know, has blessed me with a delightful and intricate conversation about literature, ethics and the world that goes back for decades. I treasure the long talks I've had with Ben Salloum, his erudition and wide-ranging intelligence have helped me understand my subject matter more deeply. Also thanks to the members of the poetry workshop group POV (Jes Battis, Troni Grande, Tracy Hamon, Medrie Purdham, Melanie Schnell, Tara Dawn Solheim and Kathleen Wall) who helped make the poems cleaner. Some others—Derek Brown, Paul Endo, Craig Melhoff, Jeremy Stewart, Dan Tysdal—have offered their wisdom when times became hard. Medrie Purdham and Melanie Schnell have been exceptionally generous during the period in which I wrote this book. Thank you to everyone.

Decades of teaching at the University of Regina have allowed me to interact with many wonderful students, too numerous to name individually. I would, though, like to offer thanks to Shelley Bindon, Jesse Desjarlais, Harjit Dosanjh, and Daniel Kemp for the inspiration of their work and conversation. The English

Department's willingness to allow instructors to develop their own idiosyncratic courses has enabled me to combine teaching with research and writing. Part of the book was composed during a sabbatical. Thank you to Dean Shannon Dea for her support of my work.

As always, I also wish to thank Jim Johnstone for his steady, incredibly generous support and excellent guidance. Jim is Canada's foremost alchemist of words. The book wouldn't exist without the kindness of Debra Bell, someone who has supported my work since my first poetry collection was published. And for her meticulous, wide-ranging and insightful, consistently compassionate eye, thank you to gillian harding-russell for her superb editorial suggestions.

Finally, I wish to express profound gratitude to Mari-Lou Rowley. Her encouragement and support for my work, indeed her continuous support of all writers in Saskatchewan, is a singular gift. So many of us have benefited from her gracious care.

Never to forget: each poem is directed to Don Coles in some way.

Michael Trussler lives in Regina, Saskatchewan. He writes poetry and creative non-fiction. His work has appeared in Canadian and American journals and has been included in domestic and international anthologies. A photographer, he has a keen interest in the visual arts and is neuro-divergent. He teaches English at the University of Regina.